TEXAS CHUCKWAGON CUISINE
Real Cowboy Cooking

By Evan Moore

© Savory House Press, P.O. Box 11105 Fort Worth, TX 76110 (800) 738-3927

INTRODUCTION

Authentic chuckwagon and contemporary Dutch oven recipes, inspired by traditional roundup fare and contributed by prize-winning cooks.

The chuckwagon traces to 1866, a seminal year in America. The Civil War had just ended, and civilization was pushing westward across the Continental Divide. In Texas the era of the great cattle drives was beginning and, in the Panhandle, Charles Goodnight and Oliver Loving were preparing to drive a herd of scrawny, Longhorn cattle more than 450 miles to Colorado.

Along the way they would create the Goodnight/Loving trail, a large chunk of history and the chuckwagon.

It was Goodnight who envisioned it, a mobile kitchen, rolling supply house and itinerant address for the men who drove his herds. His prototype would be a converted U.S. Army surplus Studebaker wagon with steel axles that could withstand the rigors of a five-month cattle drive. Inside he packed the bedrolls and slickers, the tools, the firearms and the bulk food and

rudimentary medicines that fed and maintained his crew. Strapped to a side-shelf near the front rode a barrel with two-days' supply of water and, behind it, sat a wooden box for buffalo chips to fuel a cook fire.

And at the rear was the heart of Goodnight's invention, the chuck box and "boot," wherein flour and lard, condiments and utensils, tin plates, cast iron skillets and Dutch ovens made the conveyance a "chuck" wagon.

It was a simple invention intended to provide simple fare that could be prepared on the move: tough steaks, "son-of-a-bitch stew" (into which cooks were said to throw any part of a beef except the "hair, horns and holler"), boiled coffee, quick biscuits, skillet cornbread, sometimes a little cabbage or a little corn and, always, a lot of beans.

Over time that fare grew more diverse as Goodnight's chuckwagon outlasted the cattle drive. While the barbed wire fence all but ended the big drives by the late 1880s, the wagon had become a fixture on ranches where roundups that

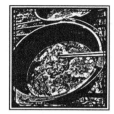

required weeks of work in the pasture were held each spring and fall. Those roundups involved branding; castration and dehorning that were performed in the pasture, far from the ranch headquarters over a period of weeks. At those times chuckwagons would be pulled to a central point and parked for the duration of the work and, with more time to prepare, the menus expanded. A side of beef, eggs, butter and vegetables could be kept relatively cool in a pit with a tarpaulin pulled over the top. Tents could be stretched over wood stoves, and baked goods and desserts appeared.

I was lucky enough to experience some of that cooking. My first experience with a chuckwagon took place on the 6666 Ranch almost 50 years ago. It was late fall and an early cold snap has spread a gray blanket across the horizon. A brisk, cold wind was moving across the plains, and the air carried a hint of sleet with the smell of wood smoke.

Shedrick Hardy III was cooking then. Tall, gaunt, skinny as a stretched worm,

he was as dark as one of his skillets — a black man who had found a seat of power in a white man's world. Hardy reigned in imperial splendor over his chuckwagon. Covered with flour and clad in worn jeans and a threadbare shirt, he stood majestically against the wind as he watched the approaching weather and ordered with authority, "Rag House." A half-dozen cowboys sprinted to stretch a tent from the chuckwagon, and Hardy turned back to his labors.

Hardy carried hundreds of recipes in his head. He never recorded one because he could not read nor write. He owned no measuring spoons and he gauged his ingredients measured by the pound and the handful. He could cook however, and that day he produced the finest food I'd ever tasted: huge slabs of fried steak sat by a pot of beans, laced with onions and green peppers. There was corn, potatoes and gravy. There were biscuits, sourdough, 2 inches thick and 4 inches square, browned top and bottom with a dense, heavy center, so laden with butter that it ran in a golden

stream if you squeezed one.

There was peach pie, a sort of cobbler with a thick, brown crust, glinting with a glaze of sugar and cooling in a Dutch oven nearby.

It was cooking such as Hardy's that made the chuckwagon an icon of the west. It was cooking that never fully disappeared. In recent years, however, there has been a resurgence of interest. Some savor the fare that sprang from Charlie Goodnight's Studebaker so intensely that they have formed groups such as the American Chuckwagon Association, a number of whose members shared their recipes for this book. Across the United States and into Canada they cook in competitions, using painstakingly authentic and meticulously reconstructed wagons. They gather in groups in the country, or they cook at home in their own kitchens.

And they've even had their own bill passed by the Texas Legislature in 2005. That group made the chuckwagon the official state vehicle.

I never forgot that meal on Hardy's

wagon. Over the years I've attempted to recreate parts of it, always with what I knew to be the same ingredients, always with authentic cast iron skillets and seasoned Dutch Ovens — and never with absolute success. Maybe it requires a cold wind and a whiff of wood smoke, the sound of cattle milling in the mesquites, the rap of sleet on a canvas "rag house." Maybe it requires an aging, wooden wagon with a chuck box and a boot at the back.

Maybe it requires Hardy.

Nonetheless, I've produced some pretty fair meals in the process and built a healthy respect for the cooks who worked with Charles Goodnight's invention. I've enjoyed trying, just as I hope you enjoy the recipes in this book.

— Evan Moore,
Meridian, Texas

TABLE OF CONTENTS

⊂⊃ SIGNATURE DISHES

⊂⊃ BREAKFAST

⊂⊃ SUPPER

SIDERS & SAUCES

BREADS

DESSERTS

It would be hard to find a more authentic cowboy than Wade Morris. A former bareback and saddle bronc rider, rodeo clown and working cowboy, he is now the official Stray Agent for Bosque County, roping and penning loose cattle off the highways there.

Morris has also won his share of awards as a chuckwagon cook. He has been eating chuckwagon fare as long as he can remember and began learning to cook it 50 years ago.

"On the places I worked, you got breakfast and supper on the wagon," said Morris. "We worked cattle twice a year, in the spring and fall. We were up at 4 (a.m.), had eaten by 5, and were in the saddle before daylight. We'd work about 650 calves by 1 or 2 p.m. and grab a sandwich or something. You were so tired by then you didn't want to eat much.

"The big meal was late in the day and we'd be in bed before dark. An old hand once mentioned to me, 'You know, there's somethin' wrong with this picture: We start while it's still dark and go to bed while it's still light.' "

"I started as a cook's hoodlum (helper) on the Jackson brothers' outfit on the Caprock (near Lubbock) back when I was 15," said Morris. "I helped other cooks throughout the years and just sort of picked it up.

"The thing is, I don't measure nothin' when I cook and I don't time it. I just throw in whatever looks right and cook it 'til it's done, so I have to stop and think about it to come up with recipes."

Morris retired from rodeo in 1980 and bought his Owensborough Chuck Wagon in 1995. He has been cooking professionally and competing since, often aided by his wife, Sandra.

His peach cobbler took first place at the Meridian Chuckwagon Cookoff in 2004 and 2005.

Signature Dishes

WADE'S STEW

10 lbs. beef (stew meat,
   brisket, or
   chuck roast)
20 lbs. potatoes
2 lbs. carrots
1/2 bunch celery

2 (20 oz.) large cans crushed or
   diced tomatoes
1 large onion
1 tsp. garlic powder
Salt and pepper to taste

Cut meat into 1-inch cubes. Cut potatoes into bite-sized pieces, or quarter, depending on taste. Slice carrots into 1/2 inch widths (or smaller). Cut celery in 1/4 inch slices. Brown meat. Add water and let simmer until meat is tender (several hours). Add vegetables 1/2 to 1 hour before cooking is finished. Will feed from 50 to 100 people, depending on their appetites.

WADE'S BEANS

1 lb. pinto beans

1 slice of salt pork

1/2 tsp. garlic powder

1 small onion

1 can Rotel tomatoes

2 tsp. chili powder

salt to taste

Clean and wash beans and soak overnight. Then drain, cover with fresh water and add all ingredients. Slow cook at a simmer for about 4 hours. Will feed about 10 people.

Sandra Morris' Hoe Cakes

3 cups buttermilk
   cornbread mix

1/2 cup sugar

1 tsp. onion flakes

1/4 cup oil

1 egg

1 cup milk

Actually pancakes, or corn cakes, these southern creations were so-named because they were cooked over a fire on the flat side of a hoe. Sandra has won a few awards for these as well.

Mix all ingredients, then cook on a medium hot griddle or in a frying pan until browned.

WADE MORRIS' PEACH COBBLER

Cobbler Filling
2 (16 oz.) cans sliced peaches
2 cups sugar
1 stick butter
1/4 tsp. nutmeg
1/2 tsp. cinnamon

Cobbler Crust
4 cups self-rising flour
1 stick butter-
  flavored Crisco
1 cup water
1/2 cup sugar

Cook the filling until it begins to thicken. (Corn starch can be added if you want it thicker.)

Cut the Crisco into the flour, add water and mix into a dough. Roll out and cut into strips and place on top of filling. Sprinkle the cinnamon and sugar on top.

Bake in Dutch Oven or in a 9-inch square baking pan in a 375-degree F oven for about 1 to 1 1/4 hours until brown. Serves 8-10.

Another group of winners who are generous enough to share a recipe or two are the Sparks family, of the B-S Chuckwagon. Bob, Nancy and son Steve Sparks hail from Brownfield and are regulars and frequent winners with their meat, bean and bread recipes.

Though she doesnt readily give up her bread dough recipe, Nancy Sparks recalls her grandmother teaching her to knead dough.

"I'd ask her, 'How can you tell how soft it ought to be?' " said Sparks.

"I'll never forget. She told me, 'Darlin', its ready when it feels somethin' like a babys butt or a fat womans stomach.' "

Nancy Sparks does, however, offer the following chicken recipe — with a bit of explanation:"The only time we had chicken around our house was when we were sick or the chicken was sick," she notes.

$tolen Chicken

1 stolen chicken	1/2 tsp. savory
1/4 cup flour	Dash of thyme and basil
1/2 tsp. salt	bacon strips
1/4 tsp. pepper	1/4 cup butter

Dredge chicken with flour, salt, pepper and savory. Sprinkle thyme and basil on strips of bacon, roll up and fasten with toothpicks. Place bacon roll in body cavity and close the opening.

Brown the bird in melted butter in skillet. Transfer to Dutch oven and bake at about 325 degrees F. for one hour or until tender. Make gravy or soup, whichever is desired. Serves 6-8.

The following is another variation on cornmeal pancakes from my own recipes - Evan Moore

CORNMEAL PANCAKES

4 cups cornmeal

1/2 cup oil

1 cup unbleached flour

1 1/2 cups finely chopped onion

1 to 2 finely chopped jalapeño peppers (depending on

strength)

2 tbsp. granulated sugar

1 1/2 tbsp. salt

2 tsp. black pepper

1 (16 oz.) can creamed corn

Boil a kettle of water.

Mix cornmeal and vegetable oil well in a large bowl. Add just enough of the boiling water to form a dough that can be made into a ball. Add remaining ingredients except for the creamed corn. Mix, then add creamed corn.

Coat the bottom of a cast iron skillet with vegetable oil (about 1/4 inch of oil). Heat over medium heat. Remove one cup of the cornbread mixture at a time from the bowl, and add it to the skillet. Flatten out the cornbread, and cook as you would a pancake.

*The following are from another award-winning chuckwagon cook,
Ranzell "Nick" Nickelson.*

*In some circles he's better known as Ranzell "Nick" Nickelson II, Ph.D., Chief
Executive for Science and Health for CTI Foods/Standard Meat Company of Fort
Worth. In the world of chuckwagon cookoffs, however, he's known as "Nick," a
former rodeo rider-turned food specialist who has won numerous awards for his
dishes.*

These, while not the winners, are easily as good:

Nick Nickelson's Pecan Pie

Crust: Marie Callender
   frozen filling

1 cup brown sugar

2 tbsp. all-purpose
   flour

1 cup lt. Karo syrup

1/4 cup molasses

1 tsp. vanilla

5 eggs

4 tbsp. butter, melted

3 cups pecans

Mix sugar, flour, Karo and molasses. Add vanilla to eggs while lightly beating.

Combine with other ingredients and pour over pecans placed in crust. Bake at 350F for 1 hour.

Nickelson's Hominy Green Chile Casserole

4 (15oz.) cans of hominy (2 white & 2 yellow). Drain but save 1/2 cup of liquid.

1 cup sour cream

1 tbsp. jalapeño juice

1/2 lb. sharp grated cheddar cheese

1 cup diced onions (sautéed in bacon grease)

10 slices bacon (cut into 1/4 inch strips; fry crisp and drain)

1 cup green chiles (fresh or canned)

Heat hominy and juice. Add sour cream, jalapeno juice and 1/2 the cheese. When cheese begins to melt, add onions, 1/2 bacon, 1/2 chiles, stir and pour into baking pan. Top with remaining cheese, chiles and bacon. Bake at 325F until cheese melts and browns.

Serves about 20.

Nick Nickleson's Cobbler Topping

Cobbler Topping (for 9 inch)

1 cup flour

2 tbsp. corn meal

2 tsp. baking powder

1/4 tsp. baking soda

1/4 tsp. salt

3 tbsp. butter

1/3 cup buttermilk

1/2 tsp. vanilla

1/4 cup sugar

Mix all ingredients, except sugar and cinnamon.

Pull walnut size portions and lay on top of cobbler filling. Cover all filling and flatten for uniform cooking. Sprinkle with sugar and cinnamon. Bake at 425F for 18-22 min. Serves about 20.

Raspberry-Chipotle Blue Cheese Dressing

56 cups mixed baby greens

4 1/2 lbs. plum tomatoes, seeded, diced

28 green onions, chopped

1 3/4 cups "Craisins"

3 1/2 cups toasted pecans (quartered)

14 oz. crumbled Roquefort cheese

Make a vinaigrette using Fischer & Wiser Raspberry-Chipotle Sauce, Tarrigon vinegar and light vegetable oil.

Toss ingredients and season to taste with salt and fresh crushed black pepper.

Serves about 40.

BREAKFAST

ᴹMICAS

4 eggs

1 tbsp. water

1 tbsp. salsa

1 tbsp. bacon drippings

1/4 cup chopped green or red
bell pepper

1/4 cup chopped onion

1/2 to 1 fresh jalapeño, minced

12 to 16 tostada chips, broken

1/2 cup grated Cheddar or
Monterrey Jack cheese

2 tsp. minced cilantro

*This Mexican dish is popular on ranches throughout the southwest and, as a
one-skillet dish, is well suited for chuckwagon cooking.*

Beat eggs lightly with water and salsa. Set aside.

In a cast-iron skillet warm bacon drippings over medium heat.
Add bell pepper, onion and jalapeño, sautéeing them until limp.
Pour in eggs and stir them up from the bottom of the skillet as
they cook. About a minute before the eggs are done, add the
chips, stirring them in well. Remove the eggs from the heat,
and stir in the cheese, reserving a little to scatter over the top.
Sprinkle the cilantro over the eggs, or serve with pico de gallo
(see below).

Serve immediately with warm flour or corn tortillas and pico de
gallo.

Serves 4.

Pico de Gallo (The Rooster's Beak)

1 cup diced tomatoes

1/2 cup diced yellow onions

2 jalapeños, seeded and
chopped fine

1/2 cup coarsely chopped
cilantro

Juice from 1/2 lime

1 pinch dried oregano

1 clove garlic, chopped fine

Salt to taste

White pepper, to taste

This is best if made the night before and can be served in a separate dish to be sprinkled over migas (or anything else) to taste.

Mix all ingredients and refrigerate the night before.

BREAKFAST PIE

1 lb. regular bulk sausage

1 lb. hot bulk sausage

1 medium onion, finely chopped

4 or 5 stalks celery, finely chopped

8 slices bread, toasted, or 3 cups flavored croutons

4 eggs

1 (4.5 oz.) can mild diced green chile peppers

1 can cream of mushroom soup

2 1/2 cups milk

1 lb. Cheddar, mozzarella or Jack cheese

In a large skillet, cook both sausages together until done. Drain off grease. Chop onion and celery fairly fine and add to fried sausage. Fry onions and celery with sausage until onions and celery are about half cooked. Pour sausage, onions and celery into a large pan or bowl. Add croutons, eggs, peppers, mushroom soup and milk. Add 1 cup cheese and mix well.

Spoon 1/2 mixture into a greased or buttered 12" Dutch oven (If cooking in the kitchen, this can be a 9" x 13" pan.) Spread 1/2 remaining cheese lightly over layer. Spread remaining mixture and cover with remaining cheese. Cover and bake at 350F for 35 minutes. Uncover and bake at 300F for another 30 to 35 minutes. Remove from oven when cheese starts to darken around edges. Best to let cool before serving so it can set up some.

Serve with picante sauce or pico de gallo. Serves 8.

CHUCKWAGON MUSH

2 medium-sized potatoes, sliced 1/4-inch thick
1 sliced onion
Water
2 cups corn bread, (approximately)
Salt and pepper to taste

Despite the infamy heaped on the name of this dish, it remains delicious. Put sliced potatoes and onion in a skillet or pot. Add water to cover. Cook until potatoes are soft, breaking up the potatoes up as they cook.

Add crumbled cornbread and additional water to make gruel. Add salt and pepper to taste.

Serve very hot. Particularly good with eggs on a cold winter morning.

This is something of a side dish, preferably served with eggs and ham, bacon or sausage, so amount specified will serve 6-8.

SUPPER

First, because of its popularity, we've included chicken-fried steak. Broiled steak was not the popular dish on ranches because stringy, grass-fed beef did not lend itself to broiling. Most cowboys preferred it pounded and fried.

Chicken-Fried Steak

1 lb. cubed or
   tenderized round steak
Black pepper
1 egg

2 tbsp. water
1 cup all-purpose flour
1 cup vegetable oil
Salt

Divide cubed round steak into 4 serving size pieces. Sprinkle with black pepper. With a fork, lightly mix eggs and water. Dip each steak portion into flour, then in egg mixture and again in flour.

Heat oil in a frying pan to 350 to 360F. Fry steaks until golden brown. Turn and fry on other side until done. Drain on absorbent paper. Sprinkle with salt.

Serves 4.

We've included the next recipe because, though similar, it is equally authentic.

COUNTRY-FRIED STEAK

I lb. round steak (*not*
   commercially tenderized).

1 cup flour with 1 tbsp. pepper
1/2 cup oil

Lay round steak on a cutting board and lightly "chop" on both sides with a butcher knife, turning 90 degrees to slightly score the surface. (This works best if the meat is very cold.) Cut into portions and rub with the flour and pepper mixture. Sprinkle with more black pepper. Fry in a skillet with oil just hot enough to brown on both sides until deep brown (will be darker than chicken-fried steak). Drain on absorbent paper.

Best served with skillet gravy.

Serves 4.

SKILLET GRAVY

Leave about 1/4 inch oil/meat grease in the skillet. Increase heat (high if cooking on a gas or electric stove, more directly over the coals if outdoors) and add three tablespoons of flour to the skillet. Stir constantly until the mixture is a medium brown. Pour in one-cup of very hot water and stir rapidly to prevent lumping. Lower heat and one cup of milk and salt and pepper to taste. If it appears too thick a bit more milk can be added. If too thin, keep cooking.

BEEF AND BEANS

1 1/2 lbs. ground beef
1 medium onion, chopped
1 green bell pepper,
   cut into 1/2-inch pieces
1 (16 oz.) can baked beans
1 (15 1/2 oz.) can Great

Northern beans, rinsed and
drained
1/4 cup tomato ketchup
1/4 cup Heinz 57® sauce
1 tbsp. packed brown sugar
2 tsp. Worcestershire sauce

In large skillet, brown ground beef, onion and bell pepper over medium-high heat 6 to 8 minutes or until beef is no longer pink, breaking up into 1-inch crumbles. Pour off drippings.

Season beef mixture with 1/2 tsp. salt and 1/8 tsp. pepper. Stir in beans, ketchup, Heinz 57® Sauce, brown sugar and Worcestershire sauce. Reduce heat to medium-low. Simmer, covered, 10 minutes, stirring occasionally.

Serves 4.

CHICKEN FAJITAS

1/2 cup fresh lemon juice

4 tbsp. salad oil,
plus 2 tbsp. of oil for cooking

1 tbsp. wine vinegar

1/2 tsp. salt

1/2 tsp. pepper

1 tsp. garlic powder

1 tsp. chili powder

1 tsp. cayenne pepper

4 boneless, skinless chicken
breasts, cut lengthwise into
1 x 1/2-inch pieces

2 green or red bell peppers,
thinly sliced

1 cup sliced onion

2 tbsp. bacon grease

2 cups tomato wedges

4 (6-inch) warm flour tortillas

In a bowl mix lemon juice, oil, vinegar, salt, pepper, garlic powder, chili powder and cayenne pepper and stir. Add chicken strips, green peppers and onion and coat evenly with marinade. Marinate for 1 hour.

In a hot large skillet or cast iron fajita pan, add the 2 tablespoons of bacon grease. Heat until grease is very hot, but not smoking. Then add the chicken, peppers and onions. Cook until the juices of the chicken run clear, about 15 minutes. Stir the fajitas often so that they do not stick.

At the very last, just as the chicken is done, add the tomato wedges and stir until cooked slightly.

Serve with warm tortillas and sour cream, guacamole, shredded cheese and pico de gallo.

Serves 4.

CHICKEN CASSEROLE

4 cups cooked chicken, cubed
2 cups grated American cheese
12 flour tortillas, quartered
1 onion, finely sliced

Sauce
1 cup chicken broth
1 can cream of chicken soup
1 can cream of mushroom soup

Layer half the chicken, cheese, tortillas, onion and half of sauce in a well-seasoned skillet. Repeat for second layer with cheese on top.

Cook uncovered for 1 hour over medium heat (about 350 F). Serves 8.

HASH

1 lb. ground beef
3 1/2 cups canned tomatoes
1 cup chopped green pepper
1/2 cup chopped onions
1/2 cup uncooked rice

1/4 tsp. basil
1/2 tsp. salt
Dash of pepper
Cheese slices

Brown ground beef; add remaining ingredients, except cheese. Cover and simmer about 1/2 hour.

Top with slices of cheese and serve from skillet.

King Ranch Chicken

The following is a standard, cooked all over the southwest and originated on the famous King Ranch in South Texas.

1/2 to 2/3 lb. Cheddar cheese, grated

1 1/2 tsp. chili powder

Garlic salt, to taste

Salt, to taste

Pepper, to taste

1 can cream of mushroom soup

1 can cream of chicken soup

2 dozen corn tortillas

2 frying chickens, boiled, then cut into bite-size pieces (save stock)

1 large onion, chopped

1 large bell pepper, chopped

1 (20 oz.) can tomatoes

Put Cheddar cheese in a bowl and sprinkle with chili powder and seasonings. Then spread soups over cheese. Quickly dip tortillas in boiling chicken stock to wilt. Layer a large Dutch Oven or a 13 x 9-inch baking dish with tortillas and add remaining ingredients in the order listed above. Bake 30 minutes at 325 F. Serves 10-12.

GOULASH

2 lbs. ground beef
1 tbsp. oil
1 large onion, chopped
2 celery stalks, chopped
2 cans red beans, drained
4 large tomatoes, chopped
1/4 cup cilantro, chopped fine
3 jalapeño peppers, chopped

1 (10 oz.) package spaghetti, cooked
1 tbsp. cayenne pepper
Salt to taste
Pepper to taste
1 tbsp. chili powder
2 cups Parmesan cheese

Brown ground beef lightly in oil; add onion and celery and cook until onion is yellow and celery is soft.

Add beans, tomatoes, cilantro, jalapeños, spaghetti and seasoning; place in a 9 x 13-inch casserole. Bake at 350 F until hot and bubbly.

Grated cheese may be sprinkled over the top the last 15 minutes of baking.

Serves 12.

CHILI CASSEROLE

4 slices bacon

2 lbs. boneless beef, cubed

2 medium onions, chopped

1 clove garlic, minced

2 (8 oz.) cans tomato sauce

1 1/4 tsp. salt

1 tbsp. chili powder

2 tsp. granulated sugar

2 dashes hot pepper sauce

2 (20 oz.) cans red kidney
   beans, drained

Cook bacon in large cast iron skillet until crisp. Remove bacon; drain and crumble. Pour off all but about 3 tablespoons fat.

Brown meat in the fat and put into a cast iron pot, covered and hung very close to the coals. If cooking inside, use 3-quart casserole. Cover and bake at 375 F for 30 minutes.

Add onions, garlic and 1 cup water. Then add tomato sauce and salt; stir in chili powder mixed with the sugar. Cover and bake at 300 F for 45 minutes.

Add remaining ingredients, except bacon; mix well and bake at 350 F for 20 minutes.

Just before serving, sprinkle with bacon.

Serves 8.

FLANK STEAK GRANDE

1/2-lb. flank steak

1 cup soy sauce

1/4 cup wine vinegar

1 clove garlic

I bay leaf

1/2 tsp. sugar

Salt and pepper to taste

Place the steak in a flat pan and mix the remaining ingredients and pour them over the steak. Place in a cool place (a refrigerator if possible) and marinate three to four hours.

Grill over very hot coals for 15 minutes on each side, while frequently brushing steak with marinade. Cut diagonally into very thin slices.

Serves 4.

HASHED POTATOES

1/4 cup bacon drippings or oil

4 cups raw white potatoes,
   sliced thin

1 medium onion, chopped

1 tsp. salt

1/4 tsp. black pepper

Heat bacon drippings in Dutch oven over a good bed of coals (or medium on a stove top). Add potatoes and onion. Stir and cook until all ingredients are heated through. Cover and cook 15 minutes or until tender.

Serves 4.

Roundup Stew

2 lbs. beef, cut into cubes

6 medium white potatoes, cubed

6 medium carrots, cubed

1 medium onion, diced

Salt to taste

Pepper to taste

Brown meat in 8-quart Dutch oven, using bacon drippings. Cover with water and slow simmer approximately 1 hour.

Add carrots, salt and pepper; cook 30 minutes more; add potatoes and onions; simmer 45 minutes more, until carrots and potatoes are tender.

Serves 12.

SHORT RIBS

2 small fresh or dried hot red chiles, each about 1 1/2 inches long, stemmed, seeded and coarsely chopped

1 tbsp. finely chopped garlic

1/2 tsp. ground nutmeg

1 tsp. freshly ground black pepper

2 tsp. sugar

2 tbsp. soy sauce

4 lbs. lean short ribs of beef, cut into 2-inch long pieces

1 1/2 tsp. salt

1 cup flour

4 tbsp. lard (vegetable shortening can be substituted)

1 large onion, peeled and sliced crosswise into 1/4-inch-thick rounds

5 medium-sized firm ripe tomatoes, stemmed, peeled, and coarsely chopped

12 oz. (1 1/2 cups) beer

Crush the two red chiles (either with a mortar and pestle, or in a small bowl with the back of a spoon), garlic, nutmeg and 1/2 tsp. of the black pepper together. Add the sugar and soy sauce, and pound the mixture to a smooth paste. Set aside.

Pat the short ribs completely dry with paper towels and season them on all sides with 1 1/2 tsps. of the salt and the remaining 1/2 tsp. of black pepper. Roll the short ribs individually in the flour to coat them evenly, then vigorously shake off the excess.

Melt the lard over moderate heat in a heavy 5- to 6-quart skillet at least 10 inches in diameter. Brown the short ribs in the hot fat, five or six pieces at a time, turning frequently and regulating the heat so that they color richly and evenly on all sides without burning. As they brown, transfer the ribs to a plate.

Pour off all but about 2 tbsps. of the fat remaining in the casserole and add the onion slices. Stirring frequently, cook for about 5 minutes, until the onion slices are soft and translucent but not brown. Add the tomatoes and the reserved chile paste and cook briskly, stirring from time to time, until the mixture is thick enough to hold its shape almost solidly in a spoon.

Return the meat and the liquid that has accumulated around it to the casserole, stir in the beer and bring to a boil over high heat. Move the skillet to a cooler place on the fire, partially cover and simmer for about 2 hours, or until the short ribs are tender and show no resistance when pierced with the point of a small knife. Taste for seasoning.

Serves 6 to 8.4 lbs. lean short ribs of beef, cut into 2-inch long pieces.

QUESADILLAS

1 (16 oz.) package
pasteurized process
cheese, cut into 1-inch
cubes
1 (10 oz.) can diced
tomatoes drained;
reserve liquid

4 cups cooked, shredded
chicken (1 lb.)
1/2 cup sliced green onions
1 (6 oz.) can green chiles
6 (10-inch) flour tortillas

Blend cheese and tomatoes in a skillet and cook over
low fire quickly (5-6 minutes), stirring continuously until
cheese is just melted; stir.

Drizzle reserved liquid over chicken and toss until
absorbed. Combine chicken, green onions and chiles to
queso sauce (cheese-tomato mix); blend well. Grease cast
iron skillet and heat over medium-high heat.

Place 1 tortilla in skillet; spread about 3/4 cup chicken
mixture over half of tortilla.

Cover mixture with other half of tortilla.

Cook about 1 minute or until bottom is golden brown;
turn and cook other side. Repeat with remaining tortillas.
Cut each into wedges; serve.

Serves 6.

SON-OF-A-BITCH STEW

No chuckwagon cookbook would be complete without at least one recipe for "Son-ofa-Bitch Stew," though it's unlikely that many readers will attempt to recreate it in true authenticity.

For one thing, there is no single recipe. For another, it's not for the squeamish. Cowboys often referred to the dish as containing everything but the hair, horns, and holler" of a calf. Cooks preferred veal for this stew. They took the best cuts of meat they had and added sweetbreads, marrow gut from between the two stomachs, kidneys, heart, liver and tongue. Brains and flour were used to thicken the mix. Whatever else was available – onions, chiles, carrots, potatoes – rounded out the dish.

On the following page, we have offered a substitute, though the purists among you can certainly include the offal to maintain historic integrity.

3 lbs. boneless beef stew meat, fat trimmed

2 large onions, chopped

2 cloves garlic, minced

1 tbsp. Worcestershire sauce

1/3 cup dry red wine

1/3 cup all-purpose flour

2 tbsp. sugar

1 tsp. dried thyme

1/4 tsp. black pepper

1 quart regular-strength beef broth

1 bottle or can (12 oz.) beer

2 large russet potatoes, peeled and cut into 1 1/2-inch slices

4 large carrots, sliced 1/2-inch thick

2 cups coarsely chopped cabbage

1 cup coarsely chopped celery

2 dried bay leaves

Salt to taste

In a 6-8 quart Dutch oven, combine beef, onions, garlic and Worcestershire.

Cover and cook over medium-high heat for 30 minutes. Uncover and stir often until liquid evaporates and its residue is dark brown. Add wine and stir.

Smoothly mix flour, sugar, thyme and pepper with one cup of the broth. Add to beef along with the remaining broth. Add beer, potatoes, carrots, cabbage, celery and bay leaves.

Simmer and cover until meat is tender when pierced. Season to taste with salt.

Serves 10-12.

SIDERS AND SAUCES

Hot Pot

3 tbsp. vegetable oil

1 onion, sliced

1 red bell pepper, sliced

1 sweet potato or 2 carrots, chopped

1/2 cup chopped green beans

1 (14 oz.) can baked beans

1 (7 oz.) can corn

1 tbsp. tomato paste

1 tsp. barbecue spice seasoning

4 oz. cheese, diced (smoked if possible)

1 lb. potatoes, thinly sliced

2 tbsp. butter, melted

Salt

Ground black pepper

Heat the oil in a deep skillet and gently fry the onion, pepper and sweet potato or carrots until softened but not browned. Add the green beans, baked beans, corn and their liquid, tomato paste and barbecue spice seasoning. Bring to a boil, then simmer for 5 minutes.

Turn off heat and mix in the cheese.

Cover the vegetable and cheese mixture with the sliced potato, brush with melted butter, season with salt and pepper and cook for 30-40 minutes (about 375 F) until the potato is cooked.

Serves 4 to 6.

Skillet Cabbage

4 slices of bacon
1/4 cup cider vinegar
1 tbsp. brown sugar
1 tsp. salt

1 tbsp. onion
4 cups cabbage, cut into 1-inch cubes
1/2 cup water

Cook bacon until crisp, then remove from skillet and crumble. Add vinegar, brown sugar, salt and onion. Add bacon and heat thoroughly in skillet. Add 1/2 cup water and cabbage. Steam until tender. Serves 4 to 6.

Sidewinder

1 (10 oz.) can hominy
1 (10 oz.) can black eyed peas

1 jar (8 oz.) picante sauce
1 cup chopped green onions

Mix all ingredients and serve as a dip.

Colorado Bean and Beef Bake

3 slices bacon
2 cups onion, thinly sliced
1/2 lb. ground beef
1 2/3 cups pork and beans

1 tsp. salt
Black pepper to taste
1/2 cup ketchup
2 tbsp. molasses

Cut each bacon strip into 3 pieces and fry slowly until crisp. Remove bacon; brown onion and ground beef in bacon drippings. Combine with remaining ingredients and mix well. Pour into 1 1/2-quart casserole. Cook at 350 F for 1 hour, covered.

Serves 4.

Arizona Barbecue Sauce

1/4 cup brown sugar, firmly
   packed
1/4 cup vegetable oil
1 1/2 tsp. salt
1/2 tsp. finely chopped garlic
1 cup vinegar

3/4 cup lemon juice
2 cups water
5 oz. Worcestershire sauce
1 dash Tabasco sauce

Mix in a saucepan; bring to a boil, reduce heat and simmer 10 minutes.

Ace High Barbeque Sauce

1 cup strong black coffee

1 cup Worcestershire sauce

1 cup ketchup

1/2 cup cider vinegar

1/2 cup brown sugar

3 tbsp. chili powder

2 tsp. salt

2 cups chopped onions

1/4 cup chopped jalapeños or
   green chile peppers

6 cloves garlic, minced

This is an old cowboy recipe.

Simmer about 1/2 hour, then puree. Use as both a marinade and to baste.

Orange Sauce

1 tsp. vegetable oil

3/4 cup chopped green onions

3 cloves garlic, finely chopped

1 (14 1/2 oz.) can crushed
   tomatoes

1/2 cup ketchup

1/4 cup water

1/4 cup orange juice

2 tbsp. cider vinegar

2 tsp. chili sauce

Dash Worcestershire

Heat oil in saucepan over medium heat until hot. Add onions and garlic. Cook and stir 5 minutes or until onions are tender. Stir in remaining ingredients. Reduce heat to medium-low. Cook 15 minutes, stirring occasionally. Makes 2 cups.

BREADS

Here, we include two recipes for sourdough starter. Not all the following recipes are sourdough-based, but several are. In place of these starter recipes, a number of good starters can be purchased commercially, if so desired.

SOURDOUGH STARTER

1 cake or envelope of dry yeast

4 cups warm water

2 tbsp. granulated sugar

4 cups unbleached flour

1 raw potato, quartered

Dissolve yeast in warm water and then mix all ingredients in a one-gallon crock. (Do not use a metal container.)

Cover with a close-fitting lid and let the starter rise until light (12 hours in warm weather, longer in cool weather). Do not let the starter get cold, ever.

After using part of the starter, add one cup warm water, two tsps. sugar, and enough flour to mix to the starter's original consistency. Add more potato occasionally as food for the yeast, but do not add more yeast. Starter improves with age.

Potato Sourdough Starter

1 large peeled and cubed
  potato (or 2 medium)

1 cup warm water

1 cup all-purpose flour

1/2 tsp. white sugar (optional)

1 (.25 oz.) pkg active dry
  yeast (optional)

In a medium saucepan, cover the potato with water. Cook over medium heat until tender, about 20 minutes. Remove potato and reserve for other use.

Let cooking water cool to lukewarm. Mix flour and 1 cup potato water. Set aside in bowl with cloth or wax paper to cover. Mixture does not have to be mixed smooth; the batter will work out any lumps as it sits. It should be in a warm place (about 85 degrees F, but not above 95). Stir once or twice a day until it smells right.

It should exude a sharp sourdough smell after 4-5 days, depending on the temperature in which it is kept. A tsp. of sugar can be added to hasten the process.

To speed the production even more you can add a package of yeast to the water before adding the flour.

As with other sourdoughs, it can be kept refrigerated, but should be used and replenished periodically to maintain its strength.

Whenever used, a starter batch should be made from water and flour (amount depending on the size of the baking) and one cup kept back to keep the starter going.

SOURDOUGH BISCUITS

5 cups unbleached flour
1 tsp. granulated sugar
1 tsp. baking soda
1/2 tsp. salt

1/4 cup cooking oil
2 1/2 cups sourdough starter
  (see recipe on previous page)

Place flour in a large bowl and make a well in the flour. Pour starter into the well and add all other ingredients. Stir until mixture no longer picks up flour. Cover and let rise three to four hours, or overnight.

Place dough on floured board and roll to one-half-inch thickness. Cut out biscuits and place in greased cast-iron Dutch oven. Set by the campfire to rise for one to two hours. Place hot lid on oven, set oven on coals, and place coals on lid. Cook until brown (five to eight minutes).

In conventional oven, bake at 425 F for 15 to 20 minutes or until brown.

Makes about 2 dozen.

Cowboy Sourdough Pancakes

2 cups all-purpose flour

2 cups water

1 package yeast

1 tsp. granulated sugar

1 tsp. baking soda

1 tsp. salt

2 eggs

2 tbsp. bacon grease or
 vegetable oil

Mix flour, water and yeast. Let sit overnight, covered, cool but not refrigerated.

In the morning, add remaining ingredients and beat until smooth. Cook fast on a hot, ungreased griddle.

Makes about 12-16, 5-inch diameter pancakes.

SOURDOUGH DOUGHNUTS

2 cups of sourdough starter
(don't forget to save a cup to
replenish your starter).

1/2 tsp. salt

3 tbsp. sugar

3 (or more) cups sifted
bread flour

3 tbsp. shortening

2 eggs

Sift the flour into a mixing bowl and form a hollow in the center. Pour in the sourdough starter and add the dry ingredients, shortening and eggs. Mix into a firm, pliable dough. Put on a floured cloth or board and roll into a sheet about one inch thick. Cut with a doughnut cutter and let rise until doubled in size.

Fry in deep, hot fat until golden brown. Remove, drain and sprinkle with granulated or confectioner's sugar.

Makes about 3 dozen.

Texas Camp Bread

10 cups unbleached flour

3 tsp. salt

4 tsp. black pepper

1 tsp. granulated sugar

1 tbsp. lard

4 1/4 cups water

This is an original ranch bread made in South Texas in the 1850s.

Sift and mix dry ingredients together. Use lukewarm water; dough is rather dry. Let dough set for 20 to 30 minutes.

Roll dough out into 1/4- to 1/2-inch rounds and cook in a hot cast iron, skillet or Dutch oven which has been greased with bacon grease. Prick with fork and turn when browned.

Makes about 3 dozen bread sticks, depending on thickness, more if rolled to 1/4-inch thick.

Pan de Campo
(Panochitas – Cowboy Bread)

8 cups unbleached flour	4 tsp. granulated sugar
8 tsp. baking powder	1 1/2 cups corn oil
4 tsp. salt	3 cups milk

This flat bread, which dates back to trail driving days, is traditionally made in a Dutch oven over a mesquite fire. It is a camp staple on the fabled King Ranch.

In a bowl add flour, baking powder, salt and sugar. Add the oil to flour mixture. Next, add milk a cup at a time. Dough should be a little sticky.

Knead the dough on a floured surface. Form 4 round rolls. Roll out with a rolling pin to about 1/2 inch thick and place on an ungreased baking sheet.

Preheat oven to 400 F.

Bake for about 20-25 minutes, or until golden brown.

COWBOY BREAD

1 package yeast	1/2 tsp. baking soda
1 quart warm milk	1/2 cup granulated sugar
1/2 cup vegetable oil	1 tsp. salt
2 tsp. baking powder	8 cups flour or enough to make dough stiff

Dissolve yeast in 1/4 cup warm water. In large bowl combine all ingredients. Let stand in warm place until doubled in size.

Grease 2 (9 x 13-inch) cake pans. Pat dough into pans. Bake at 350 F for 25 to 30 minutes or until golden brown.

Dough will keep 3 weeks in refrigerator. After refrigeration, there is no need to let the dough rise before baking.

Fry Bread

This bread found its way across the southwest. It can also be found among several Indian tribes, including the Navajo, who adopted it.

1 cup milk
1 package active dry yeast
2 tbsp. granulated sugar
2 eggs, beaten

1 tsp. salt
3 1/2 to 4 cups all-purpose flour, sifted
Vegetable oil

Heat the milk over the stove or in the microwave until warm but not hot. Pour into a large bowl and add yeast and sugar. Stir in beaten eggs and salt, then slowly mix in flour until mixture forms a smooth, elastic dough.

Cover with a towel and allow to rise until double in size (30 minutes to one hour).

Lightly flour work surface and divide dough into 12 pieces roughly the size of tennis balls, then flatten into discs. Let dough rise again, about 10 minutes.

Heat oil to level at which one dough ball rises (about 350 F) in a cast iron pot, deep fryer, or deep skillet. Fry dough discs one or two at a time for three to five minutes, depending on size, turning once.

Makes about 12 servings.

Ranch House Biscuit Coffee Cake

3 cups unbleached flour

2 tsp. baking powder

1/4 cup granulated sugar

1/2 tsp. salt

4 tbsp. butter

2 eggs, beaten

1/2 cup milk

Preheat oven to 375 F.

Combine all dry ingredients and blend well. Cut in butter. Add eggs and milk to the dry mixture, then blend until combined. If the mixture is too wet, add a little more flour.

With flour-covered hands, spread dough about 1/2 to 1 inch thick on a lightly floured area.

Spread a thin layer of filling over the biscuit dough and the remaining into a baking pan. This will be placed on horseshoes or can lids in the Dutch oven to prevent burning or sticking. Roll the biscuit dough up as a jellyroll. Slice into 1-inch pieces and place the pieces into the wet baking pan (stick the biscuit pieces together like a puzzle). Bake uncovered at about 400 F. When done, turn out immediately on a plate.

Filling

4 tbsp. butter, melted

4 tbsp. corn syrup

1 cup brown sugar

1/4 tsp. ground cinnamon

Mix ingredients and use as instructed above.

BROWN BISCUITS

3 tbsp. each flour and
  cornmeal, mixed, for
  sprinkling

2 cups unbleached all-purpose
  flour

2 cups whole-wheat pastry
  flour

4 tsp. baking powder

1 tsp. baking soda

1 tsp. salt

12 tbsp. (1 1/2 sticks) unsalted
  butter, lard, or solid
  vegetable shortening, chilled
  and cut into pieces

1 1/2 cups cold buttermilk

Combine the flour, whole-wheat pastry flour, baking powder, baking soda and salt. Cut the butter into the dry ingredients with a pastry blender or 2 knives until the mixture resembles coarse crumbs, with no large chunks of butter.

If the butter gets very soft, refrigerate for 20 minutes. Add the buttermilk, stirring just to moisten all the ingredients. The dough will be moist, then stiffen while being stirred. It should be slightly shaggy, but not sticky. Turn the dough out onto a lightly floured work surface and knead gently about 10 times, or just until the dough holds together smoothly. Roll or pat out the dough into a rectangle about 1 1/4 inches thick. Take care not to add too much flour, or the biscuits will be tough.

Cut with a floured knife into 16 equal squares. Place in baking pan and put on horseshoes or can lids in a hot (400 F) Dutch oven. Bake for 15 to 18 minutes, or until golden brown. Let rest a few minutes and serve hot. Makes about 16.

Wade's Beer Biscuits

3 cups self-rising flour
6 oz. warm beer (about 1/2 can)
1/2 cup milk

Mix into a dough. Set aside in a bowl and cover with cloth and let rise. Roll out to 1/2 inch thickness.

Cut with biscuit cutter, or pinch off golf-ball sized pieces and place on cookie sheet or (preferably) in Dutch oven. (You can avoid burning the bottoms of the biscuits in a Dutch oven by placing them on a greased pie plate and setting the plate on two horseshoes, or three Mason jar rims in the bottom of the Dutch Oven).

Cook at about 400 F until brown, approximately 10-12 minutes.

COWPOKE CORNBREAD

1 cup cornmeal

1/2 cup self-rising flour

1/4 tsp. baking soda

2 to 4 jalapeños, chopped

1 cup shredded Cheddar
cheese

1/4 cup chopped onions

1 (8-oz.) can creamed yellow
corn

1 cup buttermilk

2 large eggs, lightly beaten

1/4 cup vegetable oi

Combine dry ingredients, including peppers, cheese and onions;
add wet ingredients and mix just until combined.

Pour into hot iron skillet or 8-inch square pan. Bake at 400 F
until golden brown, about 20 minutes. Serve warm.

DESSERTS

Spotted Pup
(Cowboy Pudding)

This is one of the more authentic chuckwagon recipes. Readers will note that it requires no eggs (usually unavailable). It drew its name from its "complexion."

Most chuckwagons carried no sugar, so sorghum syrup (one cup) was used instead of sugar. If sorghum is used, use one cup less milk.

2 cups white rice

2 cups granulated sugar

3 quarts milk or canned milk equivalent

1 tbsp. nutmeg

1 lb. raisins or other dried fruit

1 1/2 cups raisins or dried apples (optional)

1/2 cup rum or whiskey (optional)

Put rice in a cast-iron pot. Add sugar and mix well. Then add milk (either fresh, whole or canned).

Hang pot over fire far enough from the coals to simmer. It may require an hour for the mixture to thicken. Then stir in nutmeg, mix well, and slowly add the raisins. This will help the mixture.

Move farther from the heat (or turn low on a stove top) and allow the rice to swell. It's ready when a spoon stands in the center.

Dried apples and raisins can be used together, and rum or whiskey can be added. If using alcohol, add only after recipe has already thickened. To convert to stove top, cook in a double boiler.

DRUNKEN PEACH COBBLER

Cobbler Crust

5 cups all-purpose flour

1 tsp. baking powder

1 cup shortening

1 cup cold water

Mix dry ingredients and add shortening. Cut in with a fork. Mixture should look like coarse meal. Add cold water gradually to make a ball. Divide into 2 balls for top and bottom. Roll out one and line a well-greased 14-inch pan or 14-inch Dutch oven. Roll out remainder and cut into 1-inch slices for latticework on top.

Filling

1 cup butter, melted

6 cups peaches, drained and juice reserved

1 cup brown sugar

1 tsp. cinnamon

1 cup granulated sugar

1/2 cup half-and-half

1 cobbler crust

1 cup juice from drained peaches

1/2 cup Jack Daniels black label

Melt butter in saucepan. Add peaches, brown sugar, cinnamon, sugar, and half-and-half. Mix well. Line pan or Dutch oven with crust. Pour in fruit mixture.

Cover top with strips of crust in latticework pattern. Bake for 45 to 50 minutes. Moisten strips with water before baking and sprinkle sugar on latticework for crispy finish.

Coffee Cake

1 (10-count) can biscuits, not
 the flaky type
1 cup brown sugar
1/3 cup vegetable oil

1/4 cup milk
1/2 cup finely chopped nuts
1/2 cup raisins
1 tsp. cinnamon

Put biscuits in bottom of Bundt pan. Heat other ingredients just long enough to melt sugar. Spread mixture over biscuits. Bake 25 to 30 minutes at 350 F.

BEAR SIGNS (OLD FASHIONED DOUGHNUTS)

1 cup buttermilk	2 tbsp. baking powder
2 eggs, beaten	1/2 tsp. salt
1 cup granulated sugar	1/2 tsp. cinnamon
1/3 cup butter or margarine, melted	4 cups all-purpose flour

In the first bowl, mix buttermilk, eggs, sugar and melted butter until well-blended.

In a second bowl, combine the baking powder, salt, cinnamon and flour. Slowly add the dry ingredients to the first bowl, stirring them together. This mix should be stiff enough to hold a spoon upright; if not, mix in more flour. Knead together lightly for a minute or so, then turn out onto a floured board or countertop.

Use a rolling pin, empty bottle or the heel of your hand to roll out dough to about 1/2-inch high. Cut out circles with a small glass and set aside for about 5 minutes.

Meanwhile, pour 1 inch of oil in a large skillet and heat to 375 F. It's hot enough when a bread cube browns in about 1 minute. Slide the circles into the frying pan and brown one side. Turn over and brown the other. Set out to drain on a plate covered with paper towels. Cover with powdered sugar and eat warm.

Cowboy Crumb Cake

2 1/2 cups all-purpose flour

1/2 tsp. salt

2 cups brown sugar

2/3 cup butter

1/2 tsp. cinnamon

1/2 tsp. nutmeg

1/2 tsp. baking soda

2 tsp. baking powder

2 eggs

1 cup buttermilk

Combine flour, salt and brown sugar. Add butter and blend with pastry blender until very crumbly. Reserve 1/2 cup of mixture for topping. To remaining crumbs, add the cinnamon, nutmeg, baking soda and baking powder.

Beat eggs and combine with buttermilk, then add to crumb mixture. Beat until smooth. Spread batter in 2 well-greased cake pans. Sprinkle with reserved crumbs. Bake at 350 F for 20 minutes. Serve warm.

Splatter Dabs

There are several recipes for these, but the author prefers the sourdough variety. (See sourdough starter recipes above)

1 cup sourdough starter
1 cup all-purpose flour
1 egg, beaten
1 1/2 cups whole milk

1/2 tsp. salt
2 tbsp. butter, melted
1 tsp. baking soda
1 tbsp. granulated sugar

Mix all and beat. Pour or ladle onto hot griddle. Turn over when bubbles form on top of the splatter dabs.

SON OF A BITCH IN A SACK

This is basically a boiled suet pudding. The origin of the name eludes historic reference.

2 cups all-purpose flour

1 cup dried fruit such as raisins

1 tbsp. baking soda

1 cup bread crumbs

1 tsp. salt

1 tsp. ground cinnamon

1/2 tsp. ground cloves

1/2 tsp. ground nutmeg

1 cup ground beef suet

1 cup canned milk

1 cup molasses

Mix dry ingredients together. Add suet and mix well. Stir in milk and molasses until well mixed. Pour mixture into a cloth sack and tie with a string. Place in a large pot of boiling water, cover, and boil gently for 2 hours.

Serve warm with sweetened milk or cream if available.

INDEX

BREAKFAST

MAIN DISHES

VEGETABLES

CONDIMENTS

BREADS

DESSERTS

WEIGHTS & MEASURES

U.S.Measures to Metric

Capacity

1 teaspoon = 5 ml
1 tablespoon = 15 ml
1 fluid oz. = 34 ml
1/2 cup = 120 ml
1 cup = 240 ml

Weight

3.5 ounces = 100 grams
1.10 pounds = 500 grams
2.205 pounds = 1 kilogram

Oven Temperature Guide

	F	C
Warm	300	150
Moderately Warm	325	160
Medium	350	180
Moderately Hot	375	190
Hot	400-415	200-210
Broil	550	288

Acknowledgments

Edited by Ruthanne Brockway, an award-winning Dutch oven cook and member of the American Chuck Wagon Association.

Special thanks to Sharon McKinzie of San Angelo for her advice and sharp eye.

To contact Great Texas Line / Savory House Press, call toll-free (800) 73TEXAS, or email, greattexas @ hotmail.com.

Consider other offerings in our line of acclaimed Texas & Southwestern cookbooks

"Small size, big taste!" – *Galveston Daily News*

Salsa! Salsa! Salsa!
Native Texan Crystal Walls offers 75 different salsas, from traditional favorites to gourmet originals and even dessert varieties. "Hottest book on the shelf!" – Bud Kennedy, *Fort Worth Star-Telegram*
SB 1-892588-05-6.

Texas Braggin' Rights
Winning recipes of the best Texas cook-offs, including the State Fair of Texas, Stonewall Peach JAMboree Festival and the Black-Eyed Pea Festival. "Texana for foodies!" – *D magazine.*
SB 1-892588-01-3.

Tex Mex 101
This handy guide makes genuine Texan-Mexican cuisine accessible to any kitchen. "From family favorites to gourmet creations – recipes from Texans who know"
– *Sherman-Denison Herald News*
ISBN 1-892588-02-1.

Championship Chili
A guide to making chili, using recipes that swept top honors at the leading two national cook-offs. Includes a veteran competitor-judge's secrets on what makes a winning "bowl of blessedness."
SB 1-892588-03-X